Glamor In Soccer History

Big Names, Big Teams, And Big Winners in Olympic Soccer

By OJ Bekeeson

Table of Contents

Introduction

CHAPTER 1 Forgotten History

CHAPTER 2 Wild and Strange

CHAPTER 3 Legends

CHAPTER 4 Big Teams, Big Events, Big Wins

CHAPTER 5 Firsts, Seconds, Thirds

CHAPTER 6 Discontinued Sports

CHAPTER 7 Forgotten Olympians

Conclusion

Stats and photos

Dedication

I am grateful to God for the ability to get the various components of this work together. It may not be a voluminous treatise, but the logistics involve was tasking I must confess. So, there's no way I could have done it without Him. My mouth is full of praise.

Acknowledgments

A tree cannot make a forest it is said. This principle applies to anything in life that has recorded success in any way. So, I want to thank everyone who chipped in positive suggestions to bring about the fruition of this book. I say thank you.

Special thanks go to Jill Stevens and Christa Ynosencio who worked tirelessly with me at different times to put the final touches to this work. Their dedication and immeasurable assistance helped to get the final manuscript to the publishing desk. I remain ever grateful.

Review

It would be highly appreciated if you could leave an honest review at the end. If for any reason you can't make it to the end, please click the button below and leave your honest review. Thanks.

Disclaimer

Images of persons used in this book are simple models and are not intended to represent real people dead or alive.

Introduction

A lot has been said about how the Olympics started. Today we'll examine some of the stories. Whether they are true or not, I crave your indulgence to pick out what interests you most and feel the glamor of the games. What cannot be discounted; however, is that at a certain point in time, people gathered together in ancient or archaic Greece for fun games. The period was the summer of 776 B.C. when the first Olympics was held as part of a religious festival in honor of the Greek god, <u>Zeus</u>. Greece was part of the Balkan Peninsula. The exact location was the Olympia, the site of worship of Zeus, king of the   gods.

For whatever reason that motivated them to organize the games must be commended. It wasn't a bad idea as the games have grown leaps and bounds to date.

It was an exciting time for participating nations as it was the first of its kind ever. You can imagine how the whole atmosphere was full of the frenzy of new things in town for the locals. Since then, qualified nations of the world gather to compete. In this event, winners are in turn celebrated by the awarding of medals. Football, then, was not included in the program at the first modern Olympics in Athens, the capital of Greece, in 1896. It is understandable because, at this point in time, international football was in its infancy. However, sources claim that an unofficial football tournament was organized during the first competition that featured Athens and Smyrna (Izmir), which was then part of the Ottoman empire. In addition to football or soccer, as it is popularly known in the USA, several other games are featured, including baseball, basketball, long tennis, boxing, high jump, long jump, wrestling, javelin throwing, shot put, gymnastics, swimming, skating to mention but a few. Running and other athletic events like relay are also part of the games today.

For the purpose of this work, I'll be concentrating on Olympic soccer as the main subject. So, for lovers of the game of soccer or football, it'll be quite interesting as I take you down memory lane to see how the game has metamorphosed through good-better-best from its inception to date. So, grab a coffee, stay put, and I promise it'll be a time well spent.

P.S. A comprehensive list of photos referred to in the descriptive portion will be presented in the stats and photo section at the end.

CHAPTER 1 Forgotten History

- ### What we know of how the game started

Just about everything in history, the idea of the Olympic games was formed in the mind of a few people. The first ancient Olympics was held in Olympia, Greece in the Balkans. The early stages of the games weren't as glamorous as it is today. It is in the sense that the participating nations, the organization, and some of the games, and costumes were to some extent still of medieval era status. What we may call the first modern Olympics convened in 1896 in Athens. The game featured 280 participants from 12 nations, which competed in 43 different events. The Summer and Winter Olympic Games have alternated every two years since the 1994 games. The 2022 Winter Olympics held in Beijing, China, between February 4 and February 20, 2022, in Beijing. The event saw new games such as skating and ice hockey added to the list.

- ### Where and why the game actually started

The Olympic games started in the summer of 776 B.C. in the Olympia city of ancient Greece as part of a religious festival in honor of the Greek god, Zeus. Other accounts insinuating its origin in

England cannot be readily verified and is a discussion for another day. Today's Olympic games are held in Athens, the capital city of Greece. The Olympic Games, which originated in ancient Greece many years ago, came alive in the late 19th century and have become the world's principal sporting competition. As the world prepares for the next round of summer Olympic games in Beijing and Los Angeles in 2024 and 2028 respectively; lovers of the games should be very expectant of good things to happen at the tournament.

- **Participating nations**

Going forward, I'll be specifically discussing the Olympic soccer games. Qualified participating national teams are grouped in fours. They now undergo the first qualifying series. The winners of one group engage the runners-up of another group. At the end of this phase, surviving eight teams now vie for quarter-finals through knockouts. Four teams emerging from the knockout phase of the quarter-finals compete for the semi-finals. At the end of the semi-finals, losers from the semi-final games will play the third-place match for the bronze medal while the winners of the semi-final games will play the final match. Whichever team wins at this point, wins the ultimate gold medal and the loser gets the silver medal.

- **Who won the first Olympic Soccer game?**

Hungary and Great Britain took the most gold medals, with each of them clinging three in men's football at the Olympics. Other nations including Brazil, Argentina, the Soviet Union, and Uruguay each had two gold medals. So Great Britain had the honor of winning the first Olympic soccer game in Paris, 1900 tournament (see Table1).

The USA has dominated the women's tournament winning four of the seven gold medals so far (see Table2). Canada, Germany, and Norway grabbed one gold medal each.

CHAPTER 2 Wild and Strange

One of the weirdest and darkest moments in Olympic history took place during the 1900 tournaments. One of the programs was the shooting of live pigeons. You read that correctly I suppose. Participants actually killed live pigeons for an Olympic event.

Another weird thing you probably will never envisage is participants clipping the fur of as many poodles as they could within a period of two hours.

In the 1912 Olympics in Stockholm, participants took part in pistol dueling without actually shooting one another. They rather fired at mannequins dressed in frock coats. These are a few of the strange things that occurred at the early Olympic games. By now you must be imagining other strangest acts that were part of the program pack of the early Olympic events. If you stumble at any that interests you, please do get back to me. Should I say thanks? Wow!

- **Costumes**

During the games, the desire for best-fit attires comes to mind. An important consideration is placed on freedom and convenience when making a selection. My research into Olympic attire dressing for the early tournaments and what it is now didn't yield much contrast. Only that there was more covering for attires then than it is now.

- **Changes and Developments**

The IOC (International Olympic Committee) decided to admit professional players into the 1984 Los Angeles games. FIFA on its part did not want the Olympics to look anything like another World Cup. So, a compromise was reached in which it allowed teams from countries outside of the Nations League and South American Football Confederation (UEFA and CONMEBOL) to field their strongest sides. However, it could only permit UEFA and CONMEBOL countries to field only players who had not played in a World Cup or who had previously played shorter than 90 minutes in any single match of the World Cup to compete.

- **Age Restrictions Introduced**

In 1992, FIFA decided that the age of male competitors be streamlined to 23 years old. Moreover, in 1996, an additional maximum of three over-23-year-old players were permitted per team. This decision by FIFA propped African countries such as Nigeria and Cameroon winning their first gold medals in 1996 and 2000 respectively.

As a result of the unusual format and the separation from the main national teams that play the World Cup and top continental tournaments, historically strong men's national teams with spectacular showings have had unmemorable Olympic records. It's notable that Uruguay, Argentina, Brazil, France, Germany, Spain, Nigeria, and Cameroon have joined the winning nations. A complete list of Olympic winners list and medals will be part of the discussion in chapter five.

CHAPTER 3 Legends

The Olympic games have produced many legends both dead and alive. I recall an age-long saying that suggests if it's worth doing a thing then it's worth doing well. In the same vein, I dare say, what is worth remembering is worth remembering well. History would not be kind to us lovers of soccer if we do not attempt to remember heroes who have left indelible marks in the games. Be informed that the phrase "as of today" used in this book in the description of individual Net Worth, is taken to mean net worth at the time of writing.

Yesteryears legends

In this segment, I'll be recognizing men who have paid their dues in the Olympic soccer world. Suffices to say that this is a random pick, and there's no particular order in the presentation.

Edson Arantes do Nascimento: Pele, as he was popularly known, was born in Tres Coracoes, Brazil, on October 23, 1940. Pele was of Afro-Brazilian descent. He was a true legend and by far the most valuable player of his time. Pele was 173cm (5 feet 8 inches) high and weighed 165 pounds (75kg). The Former Minister of Sports of Brazil is married and has a net worth of $100 million as of today.

He is 81 now and probably the richest player ever: considering the time he played.

Diego Maradona: Diego Armando Maradona was born on the 30th of October 1960, at the Policlinico (Polyclinic) Evita Hospital in Lanus, Buenos Aires Province. This powerful Argentine footballer was the best of his day. His name, Maradona, has become synonymous with 'dribbler' because of his mesmerizing 'Maradonic' moves. He possessed excellent dribbling skills, very impressive footwork, and accurate passes whenever he was on the pitch. He was the greatest football player of all time considering his unmatched exploits. He was FIFA player of the 20th Century as he was once its joint award winner. He was 166cm (5 feet 5 inches) and weighed 148 pounds (67 kg) approximately. He is late and is survived by Claudia Villafane (m. 1989–2004), his wife, and five children. Diego Maradona's net worth as of today is about $500 Thousand.

Johan Cruyff: During Johan's days, the Netherlands, a small nation in Western Europe, was one of the best in the world. With Johan implementing its new Total Football style, the Dutch country made two debuts at the World Cup finals. He helped the Dutch club win eight times, three times with Ajax for the European cup, and once with Barcelona for the Spanish League. He retired from the international scene after helping his country qualify for the 78 Cup. He died in 2016. He was 178cm (5 feet 10 inches) high and weighed 157 pounds (71 kg). His net worth as of the time of his death was $4 million.

Michel Platini: Michel was a French midfielder during his days. He was probably the best free-kick taker and finisher on the pitch. He was born on June 21, 1955, and served as president of UEFA, but was banned for some ethics infractions by FIFA till 2023. He is 179 cm (5 feet 10 inches) high and weighs 161 pounds (73 kg). As of today, Michel's net worth is $20 million.

- **Contemporary legends**

People who may qualify as contemporary legends include George Best, Ronaldo Luis Nazario de Lima, Zinedine Zidane, David Beckham, Augustine Azuka Okocha, George Weah, and Kanu Christian Nwosu Nwankwo to mention but a few.

George Best: There's a saying in Northern Ireland, the home country of George Best.

It says "Maradona good; Pele better; George Best." The man, George Best, proved that a number of times. He was rated as one of the best players in the world, which could better be attributed to his unmatched speed, dribbling ability, great balance, and goalscoring expertise. He demonstrated that he had no equality both on and off the pitch. He was known for great quotes like: "If I'd been born ugly, you'd never have heard of Pele." He revolutionized soccer and led Manchester United to the 1968 European Cup and other two league titles. He is 175cm (5 feet 8 inches) high and weighed 143 pounds (65kg). George Best's net worth is $250 Thousand as of today.

Ronaldo Luís Nazario de Lima: Ronaldo, led Brazil to its most successful outing in the late 1990s and 2000s. He was one valuable player the Sambas boys did not toy with. Though this discussion is not about the world cup; however, most of his successes happened in the world cup series. He was a goal-scoring machine who led Brazil to memorable tournament outings. Ronaldo is a retired Brazilian football player. Nicknamed "R9" or "O Fenomeno " (The Phenomenon), this incredible player was thrown into the spotlight of football and made a lot of money within a relatively short time.

He scored four goals as Brazil advanced to the final against host France in 1998. He was sick the night before the final match and was unfortunately beaten 3-0 by France.

He was named a three-time World Player of the Year, and a two-time European player of the year (Ballon d'Or award).

He ended his career with 15 goals as the leading World Cup scorer. He was 183 cm (6 feet) high and weighed 220 pounds (100 kg) approximately. His net worth is $160 million.

Zinedine Zidane: Zidane was an Algerian French player. He indeed was torn in the flesh of the Brazilians. Pundits posited that even if Ronaldo had played that final match, there couldn't have been much he could have done that day. Zidane exhibited brilliance and played ferociously for the whole 90 minutes. He was the world's best for the day, an opportunity he never had again for the most part. He was 185cm (6 feet 0 inches) high and weighed 176 pounds (80 kg) approximately. As of today, Zidane's net worth is $120 million.

David Beckham: David Beckham helped Great Britain to a few successes. Football made him famous like his colleagues. They were famous for being famous and became celebrity millionaires. Whereas there wasn't much money playing soccer during the time of Pele, modern players need only sign a contract, and they'll start reeling in millions. It can be said that 'celebrity millionaires' started with David Beckham.

He is 183 cm (6 feet 0 inches) high and weighs 165 pounds (75 kg). As of today, his net worth is $455 million

Augustine Azuka Okocha: Augustine Azuka Okocha, commonly known as Jay-Jay Okocha, was a Nigerian former professional footballer. This soccer midfield maestro was born on August 14, 1973. He featured three times in the FIFA World Cup teams. He played 73 times for the Nigeria national team, and scored 14 times within the period between 1993 and 2006. Jay-Jay Okocha was to the Green Eagles of Nigeria, what Maradona was to the Argentine national team. Simply put, he was the 'Maradona' of the Green Eagles and that of his then local club sides because of his magical moves. He played for club sides such as Fenerbahce, Bolton Wanderers, and Eintracht Frankfurt. He is 173 cm (5 feet 8 inches) high and weighs 154 pounds (70 kg). As of today, his net worth is $15 million.

George Weah: George Weah was born on October 1, 1966, and hailed from

Monrovia, Liberia. He was named FIFA World Player of the Year in 1995 the only African to have earned that honor. He's a trailblazer and scored 193 goals in his 411-game club career. He was the richest soccer player in Africa during his time. He ended up in the Liberian senate and retired as a politician. He is 184 cm (6 feet 0 inches) high and weighs 168 pounds (76 kg) approximately. As of today, he is worth $85 million.

Kanu Christian Nwosu Nwankwo: Kanu is a native of the Aro sub-group of the Igbo ethnic group. He was born on 1 August 1976 and became a professional footballer who played as a forward. His name, Nwankwo, means '"Child born on Nkwo market day"' in the Igbo language.

He led the Nigeria team clung the gold medal in Atlanta in 1996. He was an accomplished player and played for Nigerian team Iwuanyanwu National, Dutch side Ajax, Inter Milan of Italy, and English clubs Arsenal, to mention but a few.

International Career: Kanu featured in Nigeria's national team between1994 and 2010. Kanu came into the limelight at the 1993 FIFA U-17 tournament in Japan, in which Nigeria cruised to a 2–1 victory over Ghana in the final. As captain at the Atlanta 1996, he led Nigeria, knocked out Japan in the quarter-final, demolished Brazil in the semi-finals, and destroyed Argentina in the finals.

Style of play: Kanu was a slender, talented, quick, and elegant player. He had incredible ball possession, excellent touch on the ball and nimble footwork, dribbling ability, and close control, as well as flair and powerful use of feints. These traits made him a very unpredictable player on the pitch of play. Did I say he was also an intelligent player, who possessed good vision and movement, as well as being a good passer of the ball whenever it was necessary to do so? This gave him a better advantage with his timing and finishing ability allowing him both to score and create goals. Thus, he had the ability to read the game and an eye for the final ball. Some pundits have posited that Kanu is one of the greatest African players of all time, and others say he's the greatest player that ever played from Nigeria.

Personal life: Kanu is a native of Abia State, southeast Nigeria, and a member of the Aro sub-group (Arochukwu) of the Igbo ethnic group. His name, Nwankwo, means '"Child born on Nkwo market day"' in the Igbo language.

Christopher Kanu was his younger brother, and also a footballer, who played the defending position. Kanu has another younger brother, Ogbonna. Kanu is of Christian descent.

Kanu was found with a congenital heart defect, which impeded his aortic valve from closing properly; it was discovered and corrected at the nick of time. Pundits were of the opinion that he would not play again and that it would affect his career. Contrary to speculations, he made a full recovery. He underwent a second corrective heart surgery once again in 2014, in the United States. That in no way stopped him from pursuing his soccer dream.

Philanthropy: Kanu's own experience with a congenital heart defect moved him to show empathy to the world around him. Kanu set up the "Kanu Heart Foundation" in 2000, a foundation geared toward tackling the problem of homelessness. He also built five hospitals in Africa to treat children with undiagnosed heart disease and provide surgery. He was motivated to do this due to his experience with a congenital heart defect, and avail himself the opportunity to give hope back to the community that invested a lot in him. He is 197 cm (6 feet 6 inches) high and weighs 176 pounds (80 kg). His net worth is $9 million as of today.

CHAPTER 4 Big Teams, Big Events, Big Wins

There are big teams, there are big events, and of course, big wins in the Olympic tournament. It's a fight to finish and survival of the fittest for the prize gold medal. Suffice it to say, only the best team wins the gold. So, grab a cup of coffee and brace up for the next segment.

- **Big Teams**

The biggest teams assembled in previous Olympics include the United States (224), Canada (217), Russia Olympic Committee (214), China (173), Switzerland (166), Germany (147), Japan (123), Italy (117), and the Czech Republic and Sweden (116 each).

It's obvious that the United States of America has been the most victorious team in the history of Olympics basketball. The USA Olympic men's basketball team has achieved a record 16 times gold medal record. The team exhibited an unbeaten streak for the period between 1936 to 1968. On the other hand, the USA women's basketball team has also won the gold medal. However, does having a big team translate to winning the ultimate soccer gold medal? Well, let's cross our fingers and wait till the next section.

- **Big events**

Just as some small and archaic events have been removed, other big and exciting modern events have been added. Among the big events are Soccer, Badminton, Basketball, Beach Volleyball, Rhythmic Gymnastics, Rugby, Swimming, Table Tennis, Tennis, Track & Field, Weightlifting, and Wrestling to mention but a few.

- **Big wins**

In considering this section, our premise is that soccer is the highest trophy of the tournament. As we have seen, the USA has the biggest team in the tournament, but only won silver and bronze medals under the banner **of Christian Brothers College** and **St. Rose Parish** respectively in the men's category for the 1904 Olympics held in St. Louis. Instead, Hungary, Great Britain, and Uruguay have clung to 3 golds, 2 golds, and 2 golds respectively. Current defending champions Brazil has won a total of seven medals, with 2 gold, 3 silver, and 2 bronze medals. However, the USA women's category has dominated the tournament registering 4 golds, with Canada, Germany, and Norway each clinching 1 gold. Winners of silver and bronze medals will be shown in the table in chapter 5. So, wait for it!

CHAPTER 5 Firsts, Seconds, Thirds

As the title shows, tag names simply depict the order in which tournament medals are awarded to the three winning teams that are going home with gold, silver, or bronze.

- **Gold medals**

The most successful team tops the rest of the teams and is given the revered gold medal. At the last Olympic soccer games in Tokyo, Japan 2020, Brazil emerged as the overall champion as the most valuable or best team of the tournament. And as the defending champion, Brazil will be defending this same trophy at the 2024 games in Paris, France. Other gold medals for different Olympic years are displayed on a table in this chapter.

- **Silver medals**

In the same tournament, Spain being the runners-up, clung to the silver medal. If it qualifies for the 2024 Olympic games, it will be contending for the gold medal alongside other participating national teams. Simply put, it has to fight for a place to even be at the games in Paris, 2024.

- **Bronze medals**

The Mexican national team won the third-place match against host country Japan, for the bronze consolation trophy. Like Spain, it will be contending for the gold medal should it qualify for the Paris Olympics in 2024.

Below is a comprehensive list of winners at the various Olympic games.

Table 1. Men's Olympic football winners

Olympics	Gold	Silver	Bronze
Tokyo 2020	Brazil	Spain	Mexico
Rio 2016	Brazil	Germany	Nigeria
London 2012	Mexico	Brazil	South Korea
Beijing 2008	Argentina	Nigeria	Brazil
Athens 2004	Argentina	Paraguay	Italy
Sydney 2000	Cameroon	Spain	Chile
Atlanta 1996	Nigeria	Argentina	Brazil

Men's Olympic football medal winners

Olympics	Gold	Silver	Bronze
Barcelona 1992	Spain	Poland	Ghana
Seoul 1988	Soviet Union	Brazil	Germany
Los Angeles 1984	France	Brazil	Yugoslavia
Mosco 1980	Czechoslovakia	East Germany	Soviet Union
Montreal 1976	East Germany	Poland	Soviet Union
Munich 1972	Poland	Hungary	Soviet Union East Germany

Mexico City 1968	Hungary	Bulgaria	Japan
Tokyo 1964	Hungary	Czechoslovakia	Germany
Rome 1960	Yugoslavia	Denmark	Hungary
Melbourne 1956	Soviet Union	Yugoslavia	Bulgaria
Helsinki 1952	Hungary	Yugoslavia	Sweden
London 1948	Sweden	Yugoslavia	Denmark
Berlin 1936	Italy	Austria	Norway
Amsterdam 1928	Uruguay	Argentina	Italy
Paris 1924	Uruguay	Switzerland	Sweden
Antwerp 1920	Belgium	Spain	Netherlands

Stockholm 1912	Great Britain	Denmark	Netherlands
London 1908	Great Britain	Denmark	Netherlands
St Louis 1904	Canada	Christian Brothers College (USA)	St. Rose Parish (USA)
Paris 1900	Great Britain	France	Belgium

Table 2. Women's Olympic football medal winners

Olympics	**Gold**	**Silver**	**Bronze**

Tokyo 2020	Canada	Sweden	USA
Rio 2016	Germany	Sweden	Canada
London 2012	USA	Japan	Canada
Beijing 2008	USA	Brazil	Germany
Athens 2004	USA	Brazil	Germany
Sydney 2000	Norway	USA	Germany
Atlanta 1996	USA	China	Norway

It is crystal clear that having a big team doesn't necessarily translate to winning the ultimate gold medal. It simply means that whoever is in charge has good managerial ability to gather athletes together and can do better if some work is put into it. Yeah, a team's first commitment to winning is showing up to the games. I want to specifically commend the USA team managers for their great work. However, since soccer is the most singular game full of thrills and frenzy that glues the games together; my candid opinion is that the men's category is given the necessary support it deserves to excel in the Olympics and World Cup category.

CHAPTER 6 Discontinued Sports

These were sports featured at some point in the early days of the Olympics but did not stand the test of time and so were removed from the list of events. A few of the discontinued sports are presented here and by no means an exhaustive list. It is worthy of note to mention that sporting events are added, removed altogether, or occasionally reintroduced based on their international approval.

- **List of discontinued sports**

Tug-of-war: I personally recognize and like this as a childhood pastime both in and out of the elementary school environment. It was one of the events featured at the Olympics between 1900 and 1920. Unfortunately, it was discontinued after Antwerp, in 1920 in Belgium.

Polo: The game of polo is played on horseback while hitting the ball with a mallet. It was featured between 1900 and 1936. It was

summarily removed after the Berlin Olympics of 1936.

Rackets: This game is played by two people hitting the ball against the wall with their rackets. Whoever outplays the other wins. It can more or less be compared to squash. The game featured in the

1908 Olympics, but has gone into oblivion since then.

American football: Among the sports that underwent pilot scale testing was American football. However, it appeared that most people were averse to the idea of adding it to the events due to its non-worldwide acceptance and was discarded. However, the game has found a niche among the American people and has since then been a household name.

Gliding: Powerful exhibition of aerial flight prepared for the 1940 Summer Olympics. Unfortunately, that plan was disrupted because of World War II. Since then, gliding disappeared from the Olympic games.

Glidding

Why they were discontinued

Various reasons can be adduced as responsible for discontinuing some of the sporting events at the Olympics. Non-likability, as in the case of the Rackets, is one of the primary reasons. Circumstantial situations and logistics, as in the case of gliding, are other reasons. Whatever the reasons are, the organizers of the games didn't see any need to continue with them.

- **Prospect of restoring them**

Although some of the games were removed after some period(s) of appearance at the Olympics. It's interesting to note that the chances of a discontinued game re-entering the Olympic scene are slim. However, some of the disbanded games have found their way back to the list of Olympic events. Prominent among the games that made a comeback are Golf and Skeleton Sledding. We'll consider only these two as representative of reintroduced games to the Olympics.

Golf: Golf was initially part of the games in the 1900 and 1904 Olympics held in Paris, France, and St Louis, Missouri respectively. For some reasons best known to the organizers, it was removed but was fortunately reintroduced for the 2016 Summer

Golf

Skeleton Sledding: This event made its first debut in 1928 and later in the 1948 Olympic games held in St Moritz, Switzerland. It was then removed due to problems or limitations with the bob runs

(Cresta Run) aspect of the game. Shortly after, it was widely accepted and then reintroduced to the games.

CHAPTER 7 Forgotten Olympians

Permit me to digress a bit and talk about forgotten Olympians generally. Some athletes indeed paid their dues yet seem to have been forgotten. Such athletes did not win gold, silver, or bronze. They did not finish last either but were placed comfortably in the pack. These are athletes who not only compete but also are required to pass through the mixed zone – a sort of common area or what may appropriately be termed as a locker room. In this zone, though they are not expected to stop and talk to anyone, a few reporters still meet and interview some of them about their expectations or feedback from their games. For the purpose of enlightenment and the economy of space, I've picked two of such Olympians for discussion. Let's hear them out!

Winners without medals

Alexa Paganini, a 16-year-old American Swiss, is one forgotten athlete who's very proud of herself regardless. During the Winter Olympics held in 2018, in PyeongChang in South Korea, Alexa made her first debut and was placed 21st in the pack. This means she didn't win gold, silver, or bronze, but was not placed last either.

- **Just an honor**

Alexa Paganini found herself in the mixed zone (locker room) and was interviewed by a reporter. Hear her out! In her words, "To know my whole family from Switzerland is watching me," Paganini says, "It's just an honor." Though the world wasn't talking about her per se, she was delighted and fulfilled that her family was strongly standing behind her. That's powerful and raised her hope to compete for another day.

- **Creating her own history**

Mae Berenice Meite is another forgotten Olympian in the same competition making her second debut for France. She was placed 19th after the free skate. She too was interviewed by a reporter in the mixed zone. Hear her! She acknowledged it was not the best she could have done, but was proud of the opportunity to represent France in the tournament. To me, she's a prod that most forgotten athletes are accomplished in their stead. Come to think of it, she was the only qualifying athlete from her town and country that stood in for France.

Conclusion

Olympic games alternate two years Summer and Winter. Soccer Olympic games happen every four years. Many countries have taken their place at the tournaments. Many events have appeared and disappeared, with some that were discontinued and occasionally reintroduced. Although many big teams have proven their mettle, big teams do not always translate to big wins. Successful teams are known to win gold, silver, or bronze. I thank the reader and lover of Olympic sports, especially soccer. Pele and Maradona are big-name players of all time, but not as rich as celebrity players like David Beckham. Seemingly forgotten athletes do not bother much about the top three winners. They feel accomplished in their stead and are happy and delighted for the opportunity to represent their country. It's been exciting going through this memory lane together. I crave your indulgence to get a copy for you and your friend and look out for a more interesting edition of this series after the 2024 and 2028 Summer Olympics in Paris and Los Angeles respectively. With this, we draw the curtain for this Olympic adventure. And for now, it is adieu!

Now Open
Olympic torch
bearer
Staring event at the Olympic gamess

Cricket

Discontinued Olympic game

Riffle Shooting

Underwater Swimming

Discontinued Olympic game

Skeleton sledding

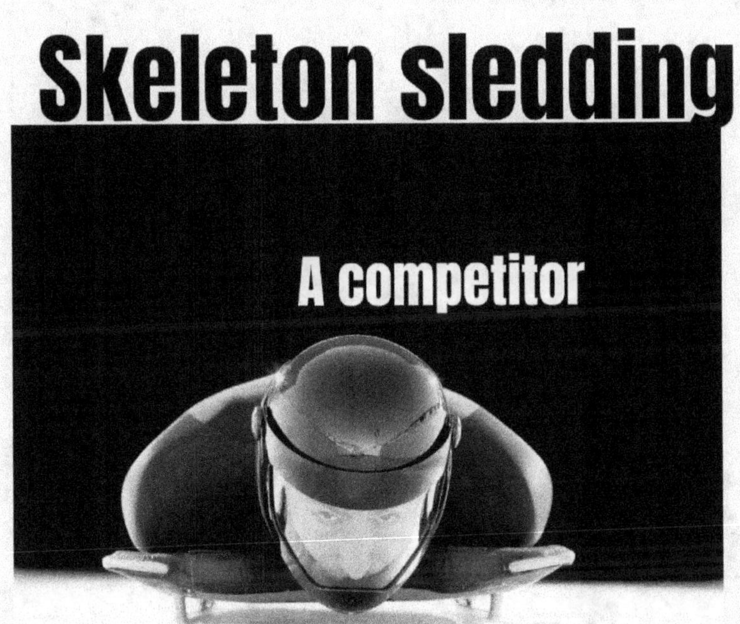

Discontinued Olympic game

Soccer Game

Wrestling

References

Bodysize. (2022). Zinedine Zidane. Bodysize.Org. Retrieved July 23, 2022, from https://bodysize.org/en/zinedine-zidane/

Canva designs. (2022). Canva.Com. Retrieved July 30, 2020, from https://www.canva.com/design/DAFGuB6LmIc/oK940vFBRRVNxWzcwkN1TA/watch?utm_content=DAFGuB6LmIc&utm_campaign=share_your_design&utm_medium=link&utm_source=shareyourdesignpanel

Celeb, H. (2022). Michel Platini Height, Weight, Age, Body Statistics. Healthyceleb.Com. Retrieved July 30, 2022, from https://healthyceleb.com/michel-platini/

Celebritynetworth. (2022a). George Best Net Worth. Celebritynetworth.Com. Retrieved July 30, 2022, from https://www.celebritynetworth.com/richest-athletes/richest-soccer/george-best-net-worth/

Celebritynetworth. (2022b). Ronaldo Net Worth. Celebritynetworth.Com. Retrieved July 30, 2022, from https://www.celebritynetworth.com/richest-athletes/richest-soccer/ronaldo-net-worth-2/

Committee, E. (2021). CONMEBOL. En.Wikipedia.Org. Retrieved July 30, 2022, from https://en.wikipedia.org/wiki/CONMEBOL

Connelly, B. (2020). How soccer has changed in the past 10 years: From Mourinho's peak to reign of superclubs. Espn.Com. Retrieved July 30, 2022, from https://www.espn.com/soccer/english-premier-league/story/4086497/ how-soccer-has-changed-in-the-past-10-years-from-mourinhos-peak-to-reign-of-super-clubs

Cummings, M. (2011). 25 Players Who Revolutionized Soccer. Bleacherreport.Com. Retrieved July 30, 2022, from https://bleacherreport.com/articles/865997-25-players-who-revolutionized-soccer

Das, A. (2021a). 7 cancelled or reintroduced sports. Www.Nytimes.Com. Retrieved July 30, 2022, from https://www.nytimes.com/2021/08/07/sports/olympics/brazil-spain-soccer-gold-medal.html

Das, A. (2021b). 7 cancelled or reintroduced sports. Nytimes.Com. Retrieved July 30, 2022, from https://www.nytimes.com/2021/08/07/sports/olympics/brazil-spain-soccer-gold-medal.html

David beckham height, weight, age, biography, affairs & more. (2022). Starsunfolded.Com. Retrieved July 30, 2022, from https://starsunfolded.com/david-beckham/

David Beckham Net Worth 2022: Biography Career Income Home. (2022). Caknowledge.Com. Retrieved July 30, 2022, from https://caknowledge.com/net-worth-of-david-beckham/

The "Forgotten Olympians": Winners Even Without Medals. (2022). Npr.Org. Retrieved July 30, 2022, from https://www.npr.org/sections/thetorch/2018/02/24/588273129/the-forgottenolympians-winners-even-without-medals

GEORGE BEST. (2022). Wefut.Com. Retrieved July 30, 2022, from https://wefut.com/player/19/17/george-best

Grannan, C. (2022). 7 Canceled or Reintroduced Olympic Sports. Britannica.Com. Retrieved July 30,2022, from https://www.britannica.com/list/7-canceled-or-reintroduced-olympic-sports

Hayes, J. (2021). 19 Discontinued Olympic Events I Can't Believe Actually Used to Exist. Buzzfeed.Com. Retrieved July 30, 2022, from https://www.buzzfeed.com/jeremyhayes/discontinued-olympic-games

Healthyceleb. (2022). Ronaldo (Brazilian Footballer) Height, Weight, Age, Body Statistics. Healthyceleb.Com. Retrieved July 30,2022, from https://healthyceleb.com/ronaldo-brazilian-footballer/

Hernandez, M. (2021). The forgotten Olympic sports. Graphics.Reuters.Com. Retrieved July 30, 2022, from https://graphics.reuters.com/OLYMPICS-2020/HISTORY/oakpedqbgvr/

Jay-Jay Okocha Net Worth in Richest Athletes › Soccer Players. (2022). Celebritynetworth.Com. Retrieved July 30, 2022, from https://www.celebritynetworth.com/richest-athletes/richest-soccer/jay-jay-okocha-net-worth/

Networthbro. (2022). George Weah Net Worth 2022. Networthbro.Com. Retrieved July 30, 2022, from https://networthbro.com/george-weah-net-worth/

Nwankwo Kanu. (2022a). En.Wikipedia.Com. Retrieved July 30, 2022, from https://en.wikipedia.org/wiki/Nwankwo_Kanu#:~:text=Kanu%20is%20a%20native%20of,day%22%20in%20the%20Igbo%20language.

Nwankwo Kanu. (2022b). BodySize.Org. Retrieved July 30, 2022, from https://bodysize.org/en/nwankwo-kanu/

Nwankwo Kanu Net Worth. (2022). Celebritynetworth.Com. Retrieved July 30,2022 from https://www.celebritynetworth.com/richest-athletes/richest-soccer/nwankwo-kanu-net-worth/#:~:text=Nwankwo%20Kanu%20net%20worth%3A%20Nwankwo,worth%20of%20%249%20million%20dollars

Olympics. (2022). Results: Latest events in each Olympic sport. www.Nbcolympics.Com. Retrieved July 30,2022, from https://www.nbcolympics.com/results

Olympics football champions - Great Britain of yore to mighty Brazil. (2022). Olympics.Com. Retrieved July 30,2022, from https://olympics.com/en/featured-news/olympic-football-winners-list-men-women-gold-medals-champions

Olympics, S. U. M. M. E. R. (2020). Football at the Summer Olympics. En.Wikipedia.Org. Retrieved July 30, 2022, from https://en.wikipedia.org/wiki/Football_at_the_Summer_Olympics

Rupart, T. (2022). Weird and Forgotten Former Olympic Sports. Howtheyplay.Com. Retrieved July 30, 2022, from https://howtheyplay.com/olympics/Weird-and-Forgotten-Olympic-Sport

Sheridan, J. (2021). MARRIED-ONA Who is Diego Maradona's ex-wife Claudia Villafane, how long were they married, how many children did they have together? The-Sun.Com. Retrieved July 30, 2022, from https://www.the-sun.com/sport/football/premier-league/1858691/diego-maradona-wife-claudia-villafane-kids/

Starsunfolded. (2022). Pele age, wife, children, biography, family, affairs & more. Starsunfolded.Com. Retrieved July 30, 2022 from https://starsunfolded.com/pele/

Tremblay, T. (2022). Edson Arantes do Nascimento Net Worth, Height, Bio, Weight, Age 2022. Thepersonage.Com. Retrieved July 30, 2022, from https://thepersonage.com/edson-arantes-do-nascimento/

UEFA Nations Leagues. (2021). Uefa.Com. Retrieved July 30, 2022, from https://www.uefa.com/uefanationsleague/fixtures-results/#/md/35037

Wallin, E. (2022). NET WORTHDiego Maradona Net Worth. Wealthygorilla.Com. Retrieved July 30, 2022, from https:// wealthygorilla.com/diego-maradona-net-worth/

Wefut. (2022). GEORGE WEAH. Wefut.Com. Retrieved July 30, 2022, from https://wefut.com/player/15/2504/george-weah

Weird and Forgotten Former Olympic Sports. (2022). Howyheyplay.Com. Retrieved July 30, 2022, from